ROCKFORD PUBLIC LIBRARY

Rockford, Illinois

www.rockfordpubliclibrary.org

815-965-9511

ANIMAL SAFARI

Crocodiles

by Megan Borgert-Spaniol

BLASTOFF! READERS

BELLWETHER MEDIA • MINNEAPOLIS, MN

Note to Librarians, Teachers, and Parents:

Blastoff! Readers are carefully developed by literacy experts and combine standards-based content with developmentally appropriate text.

Level 1 provides the most support through repetition of high-frequency words, light text, predictable sentence patterns, and strong visual support.

Level 2 offers early readers a bit more challenge through varied simple sentences, increased text load, and less repetition of high-frequency words.

Level 3 advances early-fluent readers toward fluency through increased text and concept load, less reliance on visuals, longer sentences, and more literary language.

Level 4 builds reading stamina by providing more text per page, increased use of punctuation, greater variation in sentence patterns, and increasingly challenging vocabulary.

Level 5 encourages children to move from "learning to read" to "reading to learn" by providing even more text, varied writing styles, and less familiar topics.

Whichever book is right for your reader, Blastoff! Readers are the perfect books to build confidence and encourage a love of reading that will last a lifetime!

This edition first published in 2014 by Bellwether Media, Inc.

No part of this publication may be reproduced in whole or in part without written permission of the publisher. For information regarding permission, write to Bellwether Media, Inc., Attention: Permissions Department, 5357 Penn Avenue South, Minneapolis, MN 55419.

Library of Congress Cataloging-in-Publication Data

Borgert-Spaniol, Megan, 1989- author.
  Crocodiles / by Megan Borgert-Spaniol.
    pages cm. – (Blastoff! Readers. Animal Safari)
  Summary: "Developed by literacy experts for students in kindergarten through grade three, this book introduces crocodiles to young readers through leveled text and related photos"– Provided by publisher.
  Audience: 5 to 8.
  Audience: K to grade 3.
  Includes bibliographical references and index.
  ISBN 978-1-62617-063-6 (hardcover : alk. paper)
  1. Crocodiles–Juvenile literature. I. Title. II. Series: Blastoff! readers. 1, Animal safari.
  QL666.C925B67 2014
  597.98'2–dc23
                                                        2013032375

Contents

What Are Crocodiles?

Crocodiles are large **reptiles**. They have strong **jaws** and sharp teeth.

Crocodiles live near **swamps**, rivers, and other bodies of water.

They **bask** in the sun to stay warm. They cool off in the mud.

Crocodiles spend a lot of time in water. Strong tails and **webbed feet** help them swim.

Hungry for Prey

Crocodiles are hard to see in water. They stay low and wait for **prey**.

Crocodiles eat fish, turtles, and birds. They swallow most food whole.

Some crocodiles attack zebras or other big animals. They drag their prey into the water.

Hatchlings

A female crocodile lays her eggs near the water. She guards them until they **hatch**.

19

Then she carries
the **hatchlings**
in her mouth.
Off to the water!

Glossary

bask—to take in warmth

hatch—to break out of a shell

hatchlings—baby crocodiles

jaws—the bones that form the mouth of an animal

prey—animals that are hunted by other animals for food

reptiles—cold-blooded animals that have backbones and lay eggs

swamps—wetlands with trees and other plants

webbed feet—feet with thin skin that connects the toes

To Learn More

AT THE LIBRARY

Baxter, Bethany. *Caimans, Gharials, Alligators, and Crocodiles*. New York, N.Y.: PowerKids Press, 2014.

Paye, Won-Ldy. *Mrs. Chicken and the Hungry Crocodile*. New York, N.Y.: H. Holt, 2003.

Schuetz, Kari. *Reptiles*. Minneapolis, Minn.: Bellwether Media, Inc., 2013.

ON THE WEB

Learning more about crocodiles is as easy as 1, 2, 3.

1. Go to www.factsurfer.com.

2. Enter "crocodiles" into the search box.

3. Click the "Surf" button and you will see a list of related Web sites.

With factsurfer.com, finding more information is just a click away.

Index

The images in this book are reproduced through the courtesy of: Audrey Snider-Bell, front cover; Mayer Vadim, p. 5; Minden Pictures/ SuperStock, p. 7; Aleksey Stemmer, p. 7 (bottom left); Janne Hamalainen, p. 7 (bottom right); John Warburton Lee/ SuperStock, p. 9; Ohmega1982, p. 11 (top); Reinhard Dirscherl/ Getty Images, p. 11 (bottom); Leonardo Gonzalez, p. 13; renelo, p. 15; StevenRusselSmithPhotos, p. 15 (bottom left); Lars Christensen, p. 15 (bottom middle); Naaman Abreu, p. 15 (bottom right); AndreAnita, p. 17; Roger de la Harpe/ Getty Images, p. 19; Wildlife GmbH/ Alamy, p. 21.